Suns

By the same author

The night's live changes

Suns

Tim Wright

PUNCHER & WATTMANN

First published in 2018
Published by Puncher and Wattmann
PO Box 279
Waratah NSW 2298

http://www.puncherandwattmann.com
puncherandwattmann@bigpond.com

A catalogue record for this
book is available from the
National Library of Australia

ISBN 9781925780048

Cover design by Thomas Crosse

Printed by Lightning Source International

This project has been assisted by the Australian Government through the Australia Council, its arts funding and advisory body.

Australian Government

Australia Council
for the Arts

Contents

Do not lick lid

Experience is the lazy equivalent they don't teach you,
or won't. How the squished model plane gets renovated
or reading becomes a metonym for artful youth:
a failed beehive, the days not spent
lustrously combing backyards for lost farthings,
unopened cans of Kalgoorlie Bitter,

A thinned down set of golf clubs, the coastal
variety. Wound down the window to yell something.
Anything. That's what tamed zebras are for,
riding around on — look, there's one with its casing removed,
ecstatic *rus in urbe*, sullen roadkill. We greet each other
with mild complaints about the city we live in.

Patina

I have drawn a line in the soot
and some of the particles came off on my finger,
the rest were dragged along. There would be no re-dreaming,
maybe day-dreaming, I could see blobs of colour
behind the frame, a nameless bird on an aerial,
someone was counting back from a thousand
in another language. And when the question came
it was from the person sitting next to me, the invisible one,
the pirate, and the room froze in expectation
and wake of each amazing adjective. Yes,
the city was in trouble. No, blu-tac wasn't
the solution, and could not protect us
from the wallpaper effect, or unlock old swamps.
We knew there were photographic moments happening
as our eyelashes respired and intended to inscribe
and reproduce them: something with dials,
a cold war interior where one could imagine
couples reading copies of *Oz* and sipping coffee
with a young and beautiful Marcia Langton
before the demonstration, back when
it was really cold, and rained for days.

Previous Post

red sky cast offs
to that of a deeper, postcard moon
just a flick, a screwed-off lid
of a jar saved from recycling
remaining now as a piece of sound—the one
bracketed indication of rain
not as it is but as it is collected
on a wave-like surface made of tin
the ding of a machine, a bird scuffles
just a chick, now a honk
not a goose (what would it be doing
up there?) then more scuffling
an animal hard to imagine
puppet-like—a day when it dims
"to make up for yesterday"
so you sweat inside a plastic jacket
but need it for the rain and
a siren cuts through it
to remind you of something
the previous bracket of life, twenty-five
minutes ago, unlocking the door
and coming around the side
the moving weight of cars
not hostile, not altogether friendly,
their pleasurable version of floating
around, sleep in your eye, a radio
still as a drum, porous, agreeable
and annoying, a day: a gallery
or a tram, why not both? damp
salty surfaces and people hanging
their jackets up, sighing as if the weather

were a newspaper, dangerous,
singing, ebullient outside, teeth
gritted against the weather
as others fold over pillows
go back to sleep, toast
from wood-like, two-day-old
bread: put what you don't eat
in the compost, the slighter changes
in depth or pressure,
now a gull, yesterday a magpie—
city birds, a teaspoon against
porcelain, a brush with the day, so far
so good, gathering—

Suns

degraded echo

(de Chirico?)

a white sun, nudging a post

heavy sun: velleities

hairy sun: shaking itself dry

barely an impingement, a diluted sun,
a dilated sun, egg
broken into a large bowl of soup sun

hot tea, in a clear glass: a sun like a creek that someone, right now,
is carrying a bike across

art-like sun: an installation; the sun I just went outside to see (it wasn't there)

a sun groaning, sick in bed, complaining

a sun with spikes on it. a sun with snowflakes on it. a sun

complaining of diarrhoea, heartburn, hangover,
flatulence, 'eating too much'

a sun that resembles sour soup, a sun that resembles sour soap. a
sun that resembles bone. one gross of sun.

a sun being held aloft by a pacific god. a sun of small means the skin of a sun (it doesn't have one). a sun in a jar. in the corner of my room: sun

sun on a suitcase—an empty one; on the side of a road, preoccupied

balustrade: a sun

hoary sun: barely an impingement

the air: in sun

California, pieces of fruit, bees

Uniting Church, 'not unsunny', Salvation Army, 'not unsymbolic'

Ramadan, Christmas, Hanukkah: crystals of sun

European art, sheaves of paper, the ground

Belief: sun

Here we are with a sun on the Nile, here we are with another sun on the Euphrates

On the Danube: blue paint. Nudists in the shade.

One sovereign plate of gruel, cooling on a step.

Sun on a computer, a disassembled one

Sun on a ticket inspector, sun on China

Sun on a tank of sharks, on shells,

dust, film, and boxes of money

On an airmail letter, the brown hands holding it

on a nest, a flight

on toothpaste, glue and sunscreen. Sun on a whole person at once.

on the tare weight of a truck,

a barge of sun, a tugboat towing a medium-sized sun

sun on alcohol: a breath

on metal parts: a keyhole

sun on a blood transfusion, lowering oneself into a sun, groaning - - - -

'glad-handing'; pieces of sun, at the market, taking photos of them

proof: sun

a verdict, a view

a sun—groaning on a desk

yellowing facsimile (a drawing of a sun)

sun on floodwater, sun on sandbags, sun on an ambulance

life, spokes, an exhortation

a bean, an envelope, a sun

sun on a riot squad, sun on someone's forearm, asleep

sun on the Sea of Japan, sun on the lobby of the National Institute
for the Dramatic Arts

sun on River Phoenix and on Heath Ledger, going into the sun

on Kevin Costner and on George Clooney, rowing a boat

sun on a scientologist, smoking (in the sun)

sun on a smoke machine, sun on people who speak
four languages

sun on John Ashbery, flipping an LP
at a party in the 1960s

sun on a spelunker, sun on a mail-sorter

sun on a circle of spew on a Saturday morning in South Sydney, sun on a smile
upon seeing this

sun on an iceberg, sun on a sponge

sun on a locksmith, sun on applause. Sun on people shucking corn: a decaying s

sun on dry land and on sand (that covers some of it)

a colander, a mass arrest, a serial pest -- a deckchair made of recycled suns

sun on Gregory Ulmer, he needs some; sun on Walter Benjamin

sun on Walter Benjamin in 2011, calmly reading *The Collected Poems of Ted Berrigan*

sun on Bruce Beaver in 1972, calmly reading the *Gesammelte Schriften* of Walter Benjamin

sun on the dewey decimal system

sun on the bloodbanks of Silicon Valley

rubbish strikes, velodromes, rain

consider the types of sun listed on Wikipedia, the different colours of suns
, 19th century suns versus the suns of today, organise a symposium
on this subject

between each thought: a sun

abstraction: a sun

coeval lungs: the purity and complexity of every living sun

colonial lungs: a sun keeping us 'up at night'

sun on conurbations

sun: autodidact

a sun: a contemporary

sun on colonialism, midriffs, and snuff

sun on the act of contemplation

sun on method acting, nursing homes; a long edifying essay called 'On Suns'

a sun diving into a lake

a sun driving a car into a pond

Swedenborgianism.

contours, dithering; sun on bread

sun on others, sun on 'long unexplained absences'

sun on piercings, tocsins, and electronic chimes

sun on the concealed surfaces of Gould's Book Arcade

sun on a plainclothes police, sun on a peloton

a sun 'taken by surprise' -- *still a sun*!

sun on a packing crate, sun on the sound a piece of cardboard
driven over in a car makes—'thuck thuck'

every organism is more or less a congeries of suns

                    - -

sun on organisations

refineries, furnaces: ersatz suns

science experiments, prisons, sleeping arrangements

a sun stroked like a cat, docile in the sun

a complaining sun, a raining sun

a sun leaving itself in places, it has to—it can't be helped

sun on charcoal: a blank page

camels sitting down with suns, with sun on them

a generation: a sound

a catafalque: a translation

at times, more than enough, carried home in a sleeping bag

continuously,

indivisible

suns

method napping pattern

the plane drops I start to babble
and to thai pop we're hatched into
creamy oxygen branch-snapping
the page I didn't photocopy
of a hare stamping backgrounds *fuck*
it was all on the usb another
errand stuffed up the library card carrying
traffic on the lock ashey enough until
a feeling constructed from cereal packets
under gnome supervision expanded he said
gesturing over the hedge to where past
and future selves rehearsed their lines
then proceeded through a turnstile he was
right about it I checked online but
what a weird thing to say anyway
it was all cool he kept in touch with
a distant relative of mine typing
draughty SMSs all in caps

woolly enough to stare or be
stared at took your tinsel from its
hiding spot where the pattern
interpreted correctly gave directions
to a soft relic box and made
an easter bonnet out of it prospecting
shirtless on the common drunk on pints
for stale bread to make hulls from the
cassettes were rolling but billy
bragg never passed through his accent
would've marked him a hinge of
sunlight had them out after

scrabble spelling intricate sun words
a barbecue's hiss london so far

Breakfast all day

Later he'd describe that night 'a production line of sighs'
and I'd draw a squiggly line beside it and the word
'friendship', question mark. We broke onions
into soup as a montage was projected on a wall
of different people running away from or towards
that which we were yet to know, and in which
we soon lost interest. 'Is your brother a mascot
for a certain football team?' one of them asked
slyly, and I responded with silence. A traffic light
outside coloured the room intermittently; I
had had it installed, I admitted. Nearby
was a large sign that read "Lake for Lease"—
that too was my handiwork, I told the visitor;
people were calling, wanting to know
when it would be available, where they could
download an application. As you can see
they are now a series of moons asleep on my carpet,
so we had won a kind of pyrrhic victory, I gather
others came off worse: kitschy hate mail,
whispers outside the tackle shop. What
do you expect in an allotment like
this? The paper ran an even-handed story
casting me as the loveable rogue,
and now the locals will address me by
a nickname I had as a child. By this time
the smoke alarm had been sounding for
several minutes, but none of them stirred.
'Now, then, or afterwards,' I heard a mother say,
calmly, to her daughter, one quarter her size.

All of these stories, I continued, would be folded
like so (I demonstrated), sealed with spit, and pressed
between the joists of the roof, when we became
part of that culture. It was a lewd way of saying
what we all already knew, I couldn't resist.

near accidents

"oh no! it hurts!"
— Richard Hell

there'll be no billy ocean
till we meet inside the radio
on albany highway
a bee once stung me on the nipple there
        it was classically trained
in techniques of surprise / and exited
past a future lover thru the passenger side window
to fizz out on the cut grass
in bee-eye view
of the bicentennial memorial
lake
half a line of wang wei translated
in its mind
this thing   extreme
well, this
was something new
and that night or soon
inside the shell of a car again
a soft-focus filter between us
        and the drone
of the recently deceased
that might have been engine hum or radio
but when the song came on
memory clicked in
and i forgot where i was

The nugatory heaven

The picnics played real estate on the grass
Replenishing his smile with a metal flask
The sun came down spiking the clouds in its path
Hitting the ground as in a crayon pastoral

Replenishing his smile with a metal flask
The muted parades sold their retreats
Hitting the ground as in a crayon pastoral
Indications glistened on the suburb

The muted parades sold their retreats
A nervous agent delayed his rounds
Indications glistened on the suburb
Different colours assumed the foreground

A nervous agent delayed his rounds
Betraying emollient beliefs
Different colours assumed the foreground
Brokering incautious platitudes

Betraying emollient beliefs
Drowsy feuds came to rest
Brokering incautious platitudes
Pulchritudinous scraps blew past

Drowsy feuds came to rest
The construction site was eerily quiet
Pulchritudinous scraps blew past
That indicator light has been off for hours

The construction site was eerily quiet
The sun came down spiking the clouds in its path
That indicator light has been off for hours
The picnics played real estate on the grass

The cost of lamp oil

Slowly a ferocious blush suffused Isabel's porcelain face
Father rose, inserted his pince-nez
John Junior swum out to his octopus nest
Howard nodded, went back to his plough
The idea of all those barnacles was making me tense
Robert said, "I'm going to the dump to see for myself!"
Frank said, "We've got to change with the times, father"
His son was right the price of gum may have dropped but it fed as many
       weals as ever
Kenneth gave Harvey a lollipop, the likes of which none of us had seen
"Give us lollipops!" we cried
"Make your own friends!" cried Harvey
Then, minutes before the train left that was to take Mr. Once in a While, there
was a knock at the fuselage . . .

By winter I had ceased to use any fuel
except for a small amount of margarine in my lamp to practise my teeth by
John, Frank, and Kenneth started to see less of each other than they had
      in the past
One man ploughed the soil on top of the hill
"Get lost!" we yelled
Father sobbed, "I don't want my children to be gruel"
He took the offer and the money and untied his goat
and went to see Mr. Besides. He felt hurt by his son's monkeying
around
Then, minutes before the train left that was to take Mr At Last I'm Free,
he received a letter from Kathleen or Gladys or Isabel
What did it say? None of us ever found out!!

After Francis Ponge

The weird thing is I don't wish I was riding all the time, yet bicycles have
crept into almost all of my poems. I'd like to write a poem without one, but

I enjoy walking, there is time to read lost pet notices. And as my bicycle
falls apart in real time I remember how it feels to coast, a minor moral
high ground, with arms crossed. The trail of blinking lights approaches
like a cloud of bats, women and men in dayglo.

In this taxonomy, cycling and fishing are contiguous. We cough up
paraphernalia not suitable for children under five: red light, rain slick,
burley cage. Our mottos are alternately, Fossils are Contemporary, and,
Never Look Over Your Shoulder. The derailleur is a common fossil, often
found washed up in shopping centre carparks.

How does an axle stay central? It's in your index finger on the line. A call
from your mother to come home, there is no train station at Leighton
anymore so you'll have to walk all the way back to Gosnells. The burley
will disperse and attract whiting and swim though your spokes

And now we cast out—the speed of a triple sinker over black water

Redactions

I

Tinkering with his plants. Waves of criticism came foaming in. It was never like that here before. The delusion of grammar. Frank Sargeson, typing naked in the garden. Evenly spaced piles of sand on a cool gallery floor. The tree that drops those little black bits, hurts your feet. Save us from the moneyed and sentimental.

The drive back was nice, nicer than the drive down. I was thinking of something funny I once heard. The spoiled character. The old genres. The form admits a certain anxiety. You will bump into somebody you know eventually, it's a good city like that. The woolshed in Australian fiction. A library of moving parts. Continuously moving away from and towards. Foods that look like ice cream. Rain in primary colours.

A working salad. The diary of metal parts. One leaves something, then another leaves that one. The attenuation of an idea over generations. Intersections and roundabouts I have known. A system for thinking about more than one thing at the same time. The distinct and shadowless Adelaide sun. Image of someone emptying a large container of petrol on a road. Smoke mixed with petrichor. Cold fumes. A barbecue covered in dust. The point at which it might have been otherwise is the end of each word, the beginning of each silence.

II

An orange dial. And coffee you couldn't see to the bottom of. Vagrant and contagious emotions. The product of the spaces between the words. The cat yawned. The bike tangled itself into a tree. It was a walking bicycle. The long plain that needs to be there between the forest and the agreed upon edge to the Indian Ocean.

Internal logic, cassette player. A magpie regretting last night. Shaking salt into flour. A high level of redundancy, a long table across space.

Articulated line of ants, moving along a branch. A frisbee leaves a hand as if it had always been travelling at that speed. Nothing much happens. Remove seal, turn upside down. A burning spear moving horizontally between trees through complete darkness.

III

Driving through Kwinana at night. Slight buzz of picture changing. The background of the imagination. Walking, taking parts of the ground with you.

The people wear different colours, though we can't see them, it's completely dark. Come rolling down the windbreak. Strict reply to the heretofore unmentioned. But it did happen. A learned movement that involved disattaching some parts of your body from something, while allowing other parts to become attached, then re-attaching the disattached parts while disattaching the parts which had recently become attached. Over and between pockets of air. Sleeping with windows wide open in June, sign you are becoming unhinged. Rent a newspaper. Invite people over.

Not at all a musical discussion. Inside a handsome building. The floodwater in the photograph, the surface of it. An esperanto for objects. Party on a broken tennis court.

IV

This is coming from somewhere else now, a clustered, gold-flecked shore.
Hard bits of Italian, too small to extract. And the breath resettles the page.
An envelope of sound, bracelet of stones around a tap. Large, papery-
headed flowers, too heavy for their stalks. They say,

> and especially now
> the one cash machine in town
> on the neighbour's roof
> vestige of old feuds
> places once blockades
> a shelter built for one person only
> raised high in a tree
> a funicular system
> for food, piss and shit
> permanent campfire smoke on clothes
> soy milk blooming in a plastic mug

of coffee. Sense of time passing. A ringtone loves itself. Falls out of a
pocket, years later, returns to its contributing parts on bitumen.

They bring provisions and attentions in small, resealable bags. Poppy wash.
Someone writing their thesis in a caravan. Having already begun and not
yet, a seabird's wings tucked under its body. The volume of an open fire, of
a forest after rain. No index relates. Yet to walk through it, the dog looking
back, imploring ahead. The figure begins to merge with its background,
then snaps into recognition. Hearing itself. Light from the Workers Club.

There is an alarm and a river, the differences
Silver Camrys glide through
Wet dog food sliced from a can, a missing finger
and the tablet becomes an open screen
Details of a season, speaking the same
sparkling on the coast road
where the bushwalkers are released

V

In this case a truckload, a book to understand
That which was taken from that which was contained
Playing surprise for money
A soft coalition of days or dyes, like these, punctured
Brought with them, raised among them
Remaining still while asleep, admiring
Trees and rocks, driven-into-themselves things
Sounds that die away less permanently
A person walking between trees
Admiring them, thinking 'remarkable'
Or walking between trees, begin
Somewhere around here, this place we don't know
A protectorate, a gathering, a gathering though shunned
Call off those coming towards, step out continue
Exhibits a dry knocking cry, sort of like _____
Bark gradually peeling from a tree, an indexical relationship
Punctuated, calling attention to itself, more or less a report
So that the place between is revealed, understood to be covered
Resembling a photograph seen earlier that day, printed on a page
The loud banging of ballerinas across a stage
A rehearsal, an emendation, stapled twice
Filed away, glittery mushroom avoided
The ground losing heat as the dog goes feral
Scattering wet ashes, coloured light
Blocks, embers, the last of them
Wheezing

VI

Crumbled into piles
People arrive and leave in the style
Of closed circuit TV on a split screen
If interest wanes throw a tennis ball watch it
Recede, rejecting the idea of a screen
Having returned from a stint in the country
As employed by Mike Figgis in *Timecode*
A mental browser, refreshing itself
Bark and flesh, revealing itself, cleared for burn-off
A rental property having recently left
Anonymous. The products washed up
Cracked open a can of, unsaturated
Having perfectly been rejected
Told how and when they could inhabit
Having always already sat down before them
As if yesterday was the past or only
Or a wave: a body passing through it, motionless, some water
Goes into the mouth. A broad view
Arrived at, has been here before,
Attracted by the rain, the wetness of it, the stacks of burning
Branches
That sculpted indifference, synthetic smell rising
Saying what once was is, is upon us, is clocked
An arm extending from the shoulder
To the organ of something else
A wet sponge, dull orange
Still there

VII

From a tank of water to a cup of coffee. 'Mistral duet' (toaster). Panasonic. An elderly couple at the door with copies of *Watchtower*, husband and wife, out for a chat. The different light of a Saturday. Phana-sonic. Turn the radio down too low to understand.

Nationalism is always bubbling away somewhere. That which is of academic interest. Acts of language. Electronic grizzle, 'dubby'. Black pencil. Turn on water and wonder. Printed out poems now things to do lists. Inside a house in Australia, learning the language of France. Cough with confidence and continue speaking. Cracking cans on the porch. Those interesting times of sobriety. A metallic token collected in the tray of a machine. Stretch your legs.

Boxes in the landscape. The assumptions of architecture. A different beach. The longer a trend takes to reach one. The grimy inner city becomes an idea. Patterns of light through the curtains. The Bolaño Effect. Packets of mud. Guy Maddin's *My Winnipeg*. 'I can't even begin to think of that yet'. A missing bracket, bed made of earth.

VIII

Compression: the shape of an animal running. 'My mind was
elsewhere'. Some thing, with other things pressed into it. Crushed
leaves and bad posture. Or reaching between leaves to take
something back. Respiration: an engine turning over. Next door, not
communicated. A temporary cenotaph. I had never seen a swarm
of bees before, pouring into itself like that. And the sky incites an
exclamation. Browsing as methodology. Cable car.

Toxic green. The sense of expectation, when walking very early
in the morning, that one is always about to encounter a body.
Inhale through a turbine. A senile blue. The dream washes over
the framework. Bend over backwards, catch the train somewhere
new. A place one was once questioned. Heavy ankle-length skirt.
Manufactured reply. Desiccated branch, place it in the freezer.
Dramatic postcard. Not the work but what the work implies.

Bust wrapped in cellophane; diaphanous transcript. 'Are we
becoming a nation of wimps?' A jug of beer carried across a
carpeted room. Luminous sweepings, staple remover. Drumming
on gathered materials. A casual eclipse, seen from behind. Opinion
columnist; common irritant. Chain of Ponds Road, western New
South Wales. Let the nostalgia run its course. 'Chromatose'. Having
driven through applause. A book, a beam. A drinking song, not easily
washed off. Walking on forest floor. Rushed through a hospital.
'Darkish white'.

IX

A divided track, lowering in volume until it's eclipsed. Red tongue on charcoal. Trees shaped by the atmosphere. A hand clasps a beam of wood. Your request is being finalised. Air pressure drops. Ironing board. Different airs unlocked. The effect of one superb book coming apart in one's hands. Drinking and walking. Gaunt pieces of furniture, under a white sheet.

Safe to say. Pollen in one's hair. An object moving through space. Breathless on the radio. Driving to Steve Reich's "Music for Eighteen Musicians". The concrete imagination. And the percolator joins in. Making a mistake, waving from a porch. The accent of that afternoon.

Music in translation, internal politics. The future poured into small metal cups. 'At this point I'm just pressing buttons randomly'. The birds come closer over time. The pleasurable state of namelessness. Disembarkation. Float into a different suburb. Ring bark. A field of disconstructed machines. Grass farm. The next mood trounces the last.

X

Turn your money inside out. Bloodless statistic. Woke up with sore muscles and wet shoes. A frame upon which. Degrees of confluence. Continuous beard of bees along a shoreline. The image equally abstract and concrete. Changing shirts, changing altitudes. The photographer can smell death.

Your quota of experiencing for the year. An object woken up. The line intersects the space, makes two adjacent areas. Conical shadow. Reservoir; a groove in the staircase. Fix on a vowel. Discretion. Or tearing strips off. Finishing what one started.

A familiar cannibal. Purified gloop. Sold by the shipping container. Live exports drifting past the groyne. Unexamined pages. Lit up like a shopping centre. Not all things are like other things. A layer of connectives. Old coffee, banana republic. Mental emission target. Dragging itself down a hill. Running and climbing at the same time.

XI

Land sweepings. Or trunks of former glory. Space equally devoted to.
Whimsical attitudes. Rapid eye movement. A corner of rubble. Falling into
line. Cash register, brass alarm. Set it afloat. A slideshow of well-washed
atmospheres.

Forgotten phases. Symphonic gloom. Wonder who'll be listening. Trucks
with us. Light throughout the house. Trusting a drove. The slinky harbour.
Shave off the crinkles, on top of your coffee. 'Live' from the skirting board.
Pieces in a felt bag.

A drum shelter, safely unrelated. Red string from the roof. Has gone
quiet. Electricity meter imperceptibly changing. Gravel teeth. Something
burning wetly. A capsule or frond. Raised above itself, from a multi-level
carpark. Affably unconnected to those others, now among them, forming
queues at locations. The driving home would also be visible. And this for
months.

XII

But where and what is the occasion. Walls covered with heavy
regency wallpaper. Gestures to indicate having heard. A grader,
carved in imitation—half of which was soluble. Wine decanted into
plastic water bottles. Make your house an instrument. Airier than
that. Having resumed what one started. In a room with no windows.

Fineries. The Prime Minister would not be drawn on. . . A
transaction. How many chairs were allowed. You only get one title.
And there it was, with a grain terminal interposed. Men in high-
visibility shirts in cars, watching. The breath between the breaths.

Palindrome. Soon it will be time to go out. To leave and then come
back. Driverless trains. Translucent shadow of plastic roof across
the grass. Through locks of wood. A hopeful trellis. Birthday bumps
in perpetuity. A breath of pollen across a shirt, an upper arm. The
remains, the working out across the page.

Pigeon Politics

Having an opinion on it
the crust of what was here before
becomes more rock-like, and in places, one can see them
The weekend paper falls apart like meat

Downhill skiers arrive and disappear
in shining suits, while by the fireplace
the chef and Matt Preston
serve up perfect agedashi tofu forever
in open mockery of the dialectic

THE SUN SHINES OUT OF OUR ARMPITS
a prismatic beam that feels sort of like
getting pinched all over
inside a Saturday morning cartoon

Fold-out Scenario

He isn't sure what this mist is about
nor that indifferent glob of stuff on the frame.

Just think how much dead nature you'll pass
today, one exhorts. which in sleep

fumbles around in the sketchbook-you,
as fresh meanings pile off assembly lines

elsewhere, like Certified Fair Trade berets,
and the trembling hand being drawn

in the absence of a coherent subject
is posed 'about to do something interesting' .

Balaclava

even tempered seagulls
they don't all look the same you know
reveals a shiv, follow each other over the ledge
combed down intentions, coming into the city now

apparent destinations spelled out like we're idiots
bitumen for the brain, treated air
'machines for building other machines'
theoretically they're similar
plying their pathos up and down the strip
and given our inclinations

entourage (bar italia)

as the toddler calls its defence lawyer
the art student
considers the ice bath cure
and the vodka fist

at the friday night fire-in-a-drum
linen cupboard delirium
or was it
the tiramisu-admirers
at the glass perspicaciously

warming it with their garlic breath
on the way there for
tinned lychees

deduced a mill of dandruff kitchen-scuffed
five-cent escutcheon tally
ho a walking bildungsroman
along the compost-line for your
dance moves sub wanna be

infiltrates
shop windows

starting something
fell victim to a slot machine gotta be
chirping how it came to worse than
how it came to

a poised metal teaspoon broken airport design pre-
world war one undrilled
on a white saucer award-winning

gauzey
money won't buy you a dropped gelato
taster now memento
mori wouldn't last the final lick

Press on Tattoo

He didn't weep on TV as Labor frontbenchers were known to
for tragedies
but there were rumours his tail was seen twitching away from the cameras
in the red dirt, the hot studio lights
    imploring, new wistful,
untainted by rorts past
a wettex applied to a soft layer of dust. . .
Cables slithered across the ground and out of sight

scarred mauve ten-speed

begins to break up
beneath weather
waiting to react
blooded chewing garlic
dot of thought uncorked
.. driveway buried
in earth and stones
dead bat in the bedroom ..
. scarred mauve ten-speed
majuscule the artist's fridge
teeming elsewhere
grated money salves the esteem
a console of mosses
variegated . . cleaved
beaten down
metallurgical
cleats separate the bike from me

All of the above

The debt's fierce whims
the world chided us for not knowing
a hard, knocking bird call
'old cloud'

The first of many
brought together
felt like drums of water
rolling towards you
or a huge woozy paperclip
lying on its side

Now a car detaches
two cyclists swish past
one tattoo less
meaningful in middle age

December's sugared night air cicada blend
sluggish car crash
red traffic lights timed like hearts

Coburg Sound

habit breaks down

Woolworths, light-gouged
through the carpark mist
          (Moonee Ponds)

a few sundry handclaps, thankyou mumbled into the verse

the moon loose and cold, blunted, close; near

ultrafine rain

last swim in chrome

flakes of pepper, street-worn tables

'Our famous weather'

a signal's crust

as butchers become florists. . .
ageing adolescents
rats tails gone wrong

a reef races its shadow

the ambulance losing its way

the dark outside (is everyone's)

the creek, as if urged along
pulled over rocks
reassembled

interlocking grasses

blurred recourse

I glide thru traffic like a pin

extruded tramtrack tuning fork

drum-fill from a storage shed

the wide berth of the afternoon

Recorded Message

Please listen closely
as your options
have now changed.

stars
mingle

a town
by decrees

- -

unsettled spring
unsuccessfully
displacing
winter

- -

SING THE ALARM

a branch cracks

- -

the stained stars
graded
or humorable

and the dark stars bend
or shine like chocolate!

- - - -

sun or shade
i take the table
with the chiaroscuro

written with a bike torch dragging against the page

mise-en-forehead

the lead LP
loses its husk window cracked
my arm
reproduced on the desk
a lump of matter
representing australia
nestled under papers
that bit
of bluestone
on the edge of royal parade

where was that again?
already half-gone
a face waits corposant
your anti-hippy diatribe
i get trapped there for a while
crush of distant birds

what did you think of it
when i was one of them
obsessing over
how you fluked it
off the rocks the bay
and then more water?

With chartreuse

the imagined cigarette
understands itself
to be pieces breaking off and returning to
the mouths of those 'mostly awake'
having mediated their breath
for a time a sense of stunned, dumb satisfaction in this.
In this circumstance it takes a policy to become sideways—
like a wall it can be piled up and prevent 'things'
from happening, other floors.
Glasses of grassy alcohol tilt on their hinges
and it comes out anyway,
a place called 'a place'—this is a place.
A breathing place.

a camera

. . .

minutes later

rising dust

a horizon

projected

repetitions

on a sand dune

the limited selection

admitted by a window

things have changed

the sun stored

on the walls

Camperdown

the comfort of the lecture theatre
above the implacable
crying in the U

walking through the old hospital
is this public asks one
the light places

a classical view
clotted remnants of air
strands of glass

the inner city calm to be believed
staircases address
once anchored movements

West End pastoral

the couch and the dog
are out the front with the D-lock
docked like broken ferries
someone left their porch out overnight
chewing over a block of wood
in a blanket of cut grass
fumigating the bus-stop café

abandon pencil

even tenured seagulls
dovecoted assemblies
grizzle in an interstice
what you do
for a breath
now intermittent
patent landscape
disembodied armrest
blundered to bed
in the stinging
kitchen light
early october
i abandon pencil
only slightly

coda

bracken and turners at the cusp
of our brainless correspondence oval
      on the vermeer
crinklecut of modern prizes
lathered in thankyous
coke death notices goodbyes
wondering how much fanta tasmanian pulp will absorb
in ideal conditions the doorbell ding

dongs and the snorer true to his word
escapes with the monopoly set

a well-raked excuse for family values
that we move through now like a small sympathy engine
      considering the options
      being whispered in an ear

course

in parched terms we scatter
weekends succumb screens
accrue sun blood red guston
exacta the past shore turning
the tap engages the lock the
path widens gradually
the prose parts to meet them
heterosexuality gleaming
typewriters high after rain
remain bathwater impaired
belief system years ago gilders
a darling foe escaping dialogue
grain fed process reciting
koans for money puking envy
entrenched half august floodlit
crazed planar motes come
ploughing themes the grosser
levers the slighter persons detached
a raft some operate a sparser resolve
apply brake on chordata new
spoke old gif counting idylls
sewn to shorter lengths pretend clips
graded panic has
a fang loose feudalism
in the outer heuristic
were more interesting larger
apparently singular we
learn streaming habitats
waning alcohol exhibits human
intelligent odes melted rivers the
assumption bloom dorsal

ague found agonist
christmas tazer pellucid
value participating alpine
insert tare flight believable
time carters became codicil
passengers breathable relatable coffers
some clock on plant secrets chalked
footpaths frequently walked on
resolution crops picture so inscribed
pied altitude red dozen meaning some of them
depart comfortably placidly
squeegees blink heavily coursed
palliative intended filament
pending neuter objects bourse tents
signed on grieving careers

cleanskin

illustrious your wish mine she
shifts like truckbowl of dice
foraged luckless mushy leafy
autumns fabricate altered season
shallow the door down naturally i
shouted the drumkit-me spilled
creekwaterlimbed against listing
staircase themed collect neat
treetrams the ampersand
greeting moves beachward their
bottlefish excellency sprayed
yuck colours sooner remain
on blocks clapped in green
distinction red your insistence

sundried steps

noetic license

accrue

sun \ under . fingernail

geniuses

unclip

"forced languor"

what insists

unstanding

smoking peat

sundried

feet

Slumming Waters

my muffled boomerangs
these silicon cliffs
bring small commotions
now the thought is floated
and bends around corners
bringing heavenly boredom
and deracinated sleep
is patiently assembled
into hydroponic kits
of rustling hessian
a deep humument

unsent

as the coins line up
beneath a pulse
of fresh tattoos
pianos separate
in back streets
but i was blinkered then
the aircraft bloom
and human hills
inhales on them
each one blighted
when the coins line up
years after the rent
shadows slide around
a continuous gesture
traffic lights remain green
dabbled in
the weight between objects
excluded air
exposed tunic on glass
caresses pleasant else
he supposes
the polished behaviours
settle on the lens
growing downwards
but the words adjust
teeming in their place
pianos separate
beneath a pulse
as the coins line up
each one blighted
inhales on them

and human hills
the aircraft bloom
but i was blinkered then
a continuous gesture
growing downwards
weight between objects
polished behaviours
he supposes
of fresh tattoos
shadows slide around
words adjust
settle on the glass
the heart grows downwards
years remain green
a pleasant weight
between years
forming words
the heart adjusts

Of the Outside

This tuneful malaise
I want to say appears
as a niece or nephew will
between shores
one has grown used to expecting—
I digress. The torn bread in the soup,
athletic hum and click,
deft knitting needles
across the lens and swerve
      of a prison song,
the nomenclature lifts
and names absolve.

remnants

charcoal-touched tongue
supported smoke
single carriage train cutting through the bush

when the stores fill up around september
a face against spokes
speaking the Pisan Cantos
into a stormwater drain

flow and flight
saying inshallah
freshwater police swim through bars
towards salt water

fireworks bump the air
and regular

mited light
blends a city fire

rain on pool tables
soaked stars
collective grief means
star pickets
summon a space of earth

a gain

a chopping board sky, isolate lemon wedge

flattened out earth, gradations of "letting go sky"

gariwerd distinguishable

this crouched-beside rock's
fending off

the oblique afternoon sun
that's lasted all day

a coveted battery
where thinking's talk leads

to utopia's wimmera—
vertebrae of old skyline

from an hour before
the pub's borrowed laptop

fridge-cold bottles now a memory
occasional phone box

gamble of five-cent coins
become nub of charcoal

held like a joint stub
between fingertips

wearing glasses for once
gariwerd distinguishable

morning particle

from the ground of lowered expectations
these desires appear to mask
come toothsome experiences dealcoholised
in solar flows of trust or pleasure
grassy plights, nostalgic dam levels
the printed day seen fall on it heels
sing the commodious husked hot-desk!
bundled failure and pulse of water
presently officeworks blinks krill
and sparkling tablet ground to foam, disappear

Chants

They are saying grace now, industrial dryers turning in the
laundries. Bitches Brew from nearby; tough, distracted, absorbed.
A plot of one's own, in the bookshop, a hole punched through the
day. Cleanly crossing a motorway, spools off into the miserable,
the shelved. A lightbox occurs, graduates to an adjacent fold. From
dream to bargain basement: they generally leave us alone. Capable,
as arms and tales of drawn out weathers. Flexidisc in the letterbox,
hand on the pane; the warm and the weatherless. Inkblots fleck the
creek at dusk. Experience squeezed out like toothpaste. It was that
precipitate, encapsulated. Caned, for the month. The hard work that
hurt, the leaf litter variously applied. A floating dock, here at the
edge of the abbreviated. A conch sense, nudged to a glossy career.
The function of music: speeds up the limbs. Studio light settles
over the room like a drink. Weaned off those concerns. Scoffs at the
tables. Brutal music through the walls. I forgot how long your body
was, what the weather was doing. The marquee appeared overnight.

An object turned to face you, its dust shadow cherubim. How large is
your art practice, the piles of decided junk. Mistaken for chocolate.
To the condition of rags, serve a colour. More intelligent by the
line, more rained on. It means nothing or something, more or less
if it is photographed. A machine made of feathers, moving along
the ground. Shenandoah. Ploughed the contents. The coloured
mud, drip method of punctuation. Fictional tram route following
bluestone. Becomes more painterly, is there a story. Hand stencils
overlap, kids jumping off the bridge. Fold up your wings calliope,
switch off the nebulizer. Measured bleeps, amplified ring. The
walking wizened, the mood inducing, the priapic. Who is to say.
Garlic paste, sugar bowl. Take a rest from the news, a listing delivery

streaming before your eyes. Pinions dropped into place. Slack rain. How long have we been doing this.

Faultless drip painting, organon of something. The place of green ships arriving. Less the amount crumbled into the brew. Drenched of music, fingers driven into ebony gloves. Blasted moods. Silver on red, a template. To have tried nothing carefully in months. With nihilist intent. Bruised sentiment at the bottom of the glass. Fondled phone, depraved solution. A recumbent splinters past. A rat blinks. There is so much still untranslated, cuts out a coupon impassively. Where were you when and would you have and in what sense. Freckles matter less, pockets a chilli. As one leaves another takes its place.

Suspended realism, the new year ends. Then they were expected to step under the rope. Comes in under sufferance, hair ironed down like a prize. The physical, plastic effort. Turned down trying. Or exits in the contained throes of sleep. Saying to oneself. Allowing a chainsaw to play through it. The current arrangement. Bilious music from somewhere. Set out on a café table. Brazen music; anti-pigeon spikes. The furniture performs the required solemnity. One scene dissolves into another. Paris swats the alarm.

From the centre of the crowd someone blows a cornet. Characterless. A rubber band or a mind magnet. Which one was found to be augmented and then why. I am all for, the door was carefully closed. A cover might describe it, a book of returns. A hoop looses itself contemplatively, skittles to the path. A right arm reaches from a car, a bended elbow. The periphery spills across aviator sunglasses. Previously on this tabletop was found. Lobbed

74

over a fence, embedded theme from MASH. Throwing money around. These levers and dials are merely decorative of course. Marinated ten cent coins, the dog-leg at the bottom of Pyrmont Bridge Road. With a red stalk and a tiny body. Chez the house with the diving board.

Important to see that as part of it too. Ground like a dream, siphoned off the contents. To the degree of the guiltless. Outside the meeting, the coleslaw exploded. Rehearsed versions of the same. Two bells sounded. The streets became more coastal, more flinty. It was that which could be left overnight that mattered. Oily cool of a mechanics in summer. Swift emblem, dragged into place. There was the curious and the space for the curious. They were encouraged to co-exist. Changes the music, brings its own borrowed regard. Crushed spot of turmeric. A description waiting to be applied. Memory of two years ago, a cogent life. Fan out over the dunes. Here the sparkling asphalt, there the mooted renewal. Weak beer and water. I have not left there properly yet. Thrown out by the eyes Because you say it is happening, the cursor docked. Careenage, come lurching through waves. This is how we play disregard. The high, cirrus effect. By which was made possible.

Dug up drumkit, dusted off. Listen, it plays fine. Our work here is tolerated. Come to grief. Imbued colour, while queuing. We pretend to know what for, hold out forearms and compare pigmentation. Drifts into the sun, the external parts to the sun. Walking through smoke, more like fur. Four blue tents on a basketball court. Pragmatism turns the engine over. That bit between, trafficked. Coke and kohl black. A sent, regarded flux, at the station of aches, a lark. Above the weekend markets, a raft instructed. Muslin over the soak. Slide the tablet across. For an aspect, wait it gets worse.

Traffic stumps, fallow. In the mushy stacks, a thin film silvers off obsequiously against fingers. Run and trouble. Felt large, rectangular, pneumatic. Comes against the or and. Water over rocks, a statement. I am also. Courses encourage, made biddable. Returns more bitterly. Follow any idea to its issue. Quotes the animal. Fissioned, metrical material, shaken over tongues. Coughing for once. Both new and normal. What it bumps against. In English please. Carrying sacks of rice. Windsock ebola. The carrion comes back to life. Grow your own laws, scraped across a crumpet, measuring precisely Thoreau. Money in the scarf pizzicato. The limpets collectible; gravel and mezcal.

Cousins . . . act differently. When in period costume. The breakdancers, afterwards. Wings detached, stupid window. All inclusive vernacular. Walk calmly to the ending. It's the obvious thing needs clearing. They make a claim, spat out toothpaste on the leaves. A jackhammer across the lake, a shiver river. Drop like fruit bats. Someone once known shaves past like a train. Collect the set. Drive through culture. U-lock placed around the neck. The machinery was chuffed, upped stumps, floated off somewhere else. The winter of not doing much, deriving shells from words. Not quite right, redact. External life awaits. Bins lined up like police.

(October-November 2011)

Acknowledgements

Otoliths, Cordite, Rabbit, Jacket, foam:e, Mascara, E•ratio, Yellow Field, Lichtungen, The Age, The Sun Herald, Dinner, Jacket2, and the anthology *Outcrop.* A number of poems also appeared in the chapbook *Weekend's end* and another untitled chapbook.

www.ingramcontent.com/pod-product-compliance
Lightning Source LLC
Chambersburg PA
CBHW030855090426
42737CB00009B/1237